Model Boat Building Made Simple

Steve Rogers and
Patricia Staby-Rogers

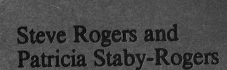
Schiffer Publishing Ltd

4880 Lower Valley Road, Atglen, PA 19310 USA

Dedication
To Bruce Phillipson, who has been a good friend for a long time.

Back cover drawing: Final resting place.
Inside back cover: Hoopers Island Drake Trail.

Copyright © 1992 by Steven Rogers and Patricia Staby-Rogers.
Library of Congress Catalog Number: 91-67007.

ISBN: 978-0-88740-388-0
Printed in China

For our complete selection of fine books on this and related subjects, please visit our website at **www.schifferbooks.com**. You may also write for a free catalog.

Published by Schiffer Publishing, Ltd.
4880 Lower Valley Road
Atglen, PA 19310
Phone: (610) 593-1777; Fax: (610) 593-2002
E-mail: Info@schifferbooks.com

For our complete selection of fine books on this and related subjects, please visit our website at www.schifferbooks.com. You may also write for a free catalog.

This book may be purchased from the publisher. Please try your bookstore first.

If you have an idea for a book, please contact us at proposals@schifferbooks.com.

Contents

Introduction

A few years ago I participated in a Wildfowl Carving Show in Annapolis, Maryland. It was held during a cold, rainy weekend in January. All of the exhibitors were either carvers or flat-work artists; I was the only ship modeler. I had recently completed a commission for a new museum at St. Clements Island for their local boat, called a "Potomac dory." Superficially, it has the appearance of a bay boat but its construction is completely different in that it has frames, and fore and aft planking on the bottom. No plans of these boats ever existed, and there were never very many Potomac dories. They were unique to the Potomac River area. Fortunately, the museum people had one, and a friend and I were able to take pictures and measurements of the actual boat.

It took me about two months to get it done and I had it with me at this particular show, a short time before I planned to deliver it to the museum.

I was talking about one of my models with another person when I noticed, out of the corner of my eye, a well-dressed, frail, elderly woman intently examining the Potomac dory. She seemed fascinated by it. After the other person left, she turned to me and asked if I had built it. Then she turned back to the boat and gestured to me. She pointed to the threshold of the cabin door and said, "When I was a little girl, my grandfather took me to Baltimore in this boat and during the trip I sat right here." I've never forgotten that incident.

It seems strange that, in these days of fiberglass boats that resemble intergalactic spacecraft more than boats, we are only one generation removed from people who actively worked in and with wood boats. Many old workboats still exist today, not to the extent that they once did, but certainly in enough numbers to indicate the durability of their designs and materials. I suppose in time they will fade from existence, taken up creeks to rot away on mudbanks or burned on the back lots of marinas to make way for more boat-storage sheds.

To some of us, the skill and craftsmanship of the builders who made them will never be forgotten. There is a talent that borders on art in creating a wooden hull from straight pieces of lumber. Even the old derelict boats are interesting because you can see the complex framing and support system that defines the shape of the boat.

This, then, is the appeal to me in making models of these old wood boats—an appreciation for the design and construction plus a gentle nostalgia for the times that these boats represent.

Materials

All of the materials you need to make these ship models can be bought at hobby shops, lumber yards, and hardware stores. Sometimes it takes a bit of sleuthing to find exactly what you need but overall the things you need are pretty straightforward and can be readily found.

Wood

Pine lumber in board form should be bought from a lumber company. Look for fine-grained, light-weight boards with a straight grain. Avoid boards with many swirls and knots. Generally, a 4 foot, 1 x 6 board provides enough material for a medium-sized boat.

You will cut the board with a table saw to form the planks, timber, and framing of your boat.

Sugar pine is an ideal material for model boat building because its general characteristics make it easy to cut and shape. I use it for wider boards and planks and it has the same general applications as pine but its fine grain allows it to be carved more easily. It can be bought in thickness greater than 3/4" up to 16 quarters, thus allowing you to cut fairly wide pieces with edge grain. Sugar pine usually has to be bought at an older service-oriented lumber company. The national chains usually don't bother to stock it because of insufficient demand.

Bass wood is a soft, fine-grained hardwood that I use for small, fine trim, like that around windows and portholes, and the coaming around the cockpit. It is available at most hobby and craft stores in pre-cut dimensions and lengths. Only a small quantity is needed for most boat models.

Aircraft grade plywood is extremely thin plywood used in model airplanes, which can be used in boat modeling also. It is available at most hobby stores in various sized panels as thin as 1/64". Usually made of birch, these panels are extremely hard to cut with a knife and normally must be sawn or cut with sheet metal shears. Some skiffs and workboats are made entirely of plywood. I use plywood for the deck and cabin structures on my models. A small amount of plywood will do.

NORMAL
BOARD
LUMBER

FACE GRAIN   EDGE GRAIN

Glue and Adhesives

The best glue for building ship models is aliphatic resin, which is readily available at lumber yards and hardware stores. The two most common brands are Elmer's Woodworking glue and Franklin's Tight-bond. There may be others but I have had success with both of these. They are water soluble which means that you can easily clean up excess glue on your model and your hands. Since they are not water-proof, do not use them on models that you intend to immerse in water. Properly mated joints are stronger than the wood itself.

Cyano-acrylic glues are marketed under the names of Super Glue, Crazy Glue, Zap-Gap, etc., and are extremely strong, instant-holding, and waterproof, but, as the name implies, are also dangerous. The fumes are irritating to say the least and because an almost instand bond occurs, extreme care must be used. I use cyano-acrylic glues to bind metal to wood, as when I install rudder hinge pins and sheet travelers on sailing craft. These glues can be purchased at hobby and craft stores; the best kinds are the ones thickened for use with wood and leather because they have the ability to fill uneven spaces. There is a line of cyano-acrylic glues designed for model airplane repairs that are available in one and two ounce bottles and are ideal for model boats. The small size is easy to handle and the glue lasts longer because the container is easily resealable.

Masking tape is used to hold two pieces of wood together temporarily and also to mask off areas to be painted. I like the 3/4" width. It can be bought just about anywhere.

Fasteners

Fasteners refer to brads, nails, and sequin pins. Brads have a smaller head than a nail and can be driven below the surface so they are invisible when the boat is finished. Brads can also be driven in one side and, after the glued joint has dried and set, can be pulled through the other side with minimum damage. The limitation of a brad is that it does not have the power to hold a plank or board that is under considerable tension. Nails, because of their wide heads, hold together a joint where stress is involved until the glue in the joint has reached its full holding power. The large heads of nails make them appear to be out of scale on a model boat and, therefore, they have to be removed. Sequin pins are used to hold extremely fine and thin pieces of wood. They do not have a lot of holding power but are useful because they generally do not split the wood and can often be left in the model. Their resemblance to a carriage bolt, a common marine fastener, adds an authentic look. The brad and nail sizes most useful for model building are from 1/2" to 1" and in gauges from 20 to 17. Avoid galvanized nails and brads because they are extremely difficult to drive. Sequin pins in the 1/2" and 3/4" sizes are the most useful and can be bought at fabric and variety stores. The 1/2" x 20 gauge brad is what I use the most, but it is also the most difficult to find. Again, check the older, service-oriented, well-stocked hardware store. They may have to be special ordered.

Brads, nails, and pins basically serve the purpose of temporarily fastening a joint together until the glue dries. Rarely, if ever, are they the primary means of holding the joint together. They merely serve the purpose of a clamp. Another useful clamping device is the spring-type clamp of which you will need about a dozen or more. The lowly wooden spring-type clothespin also does a splendid job and is readily available at a modest price.

Tools

You really do not need lots of exotic tools to produce a fine looking boat model. Mine are basic. Just keep your eyes open when you are in the hardware, hobby, or lumber store and pretty soon you will accumulate all that you need. I have learned a few ideas about which tools are the most useful, and will pass some tips on to you.

The basic carving knife that I like is made by Exacto. The knife handles are available in several different styles and I strongly recommend the style that gives you a good, solid grip. Safe and precise work depends on firm control of the cutting edge. The palm or hexagonal shaped handles give the control needed. I use a large number 2 Exacto blade the most. It seems to last longer than the other available styles.

I frequently also use a fine toothed hand saw. There are several kinds available but I prefer my Japanese veneer saw. It cuts on the pull stroke, which gives a more accurate and straight cut. I have been using one for ten years and have cut through everything up to and including steel nails and although it is not as sharp as it used to be, I still use it all of the time. They are somewhat hard to find and you will probably have to order one from a fine woodworking tool company. It is well worth the effort and investment.

Although I have a tack hammer, I drive most of my brads with a pair of needle-nose pliers. I have found that you will have much better luck and ruin less work if you spend the money to buy the better grade of needle-nose pliers. When I buy a pair, I look to see that there is a tooth at the end of the jaw. This is important when you want to grasp the head of a nail to remove it. If the first gripping tooth is too far back from the end of the jaw it will result in a large depression in the surface of the wood that will be hard to remove.

I have tried a lot of different styles of circular saw blades for my table saw, trying to get a very smooth cut when ripping lumber for my models. I have had the best luck with the hollow groundplaner blade. Although difficult to square, it yields the finest surface with the least amount of friction and heat build-up. This blade allows me to cut wood strips as thin as 3/32 of an inch that requires little, if any, sanding.

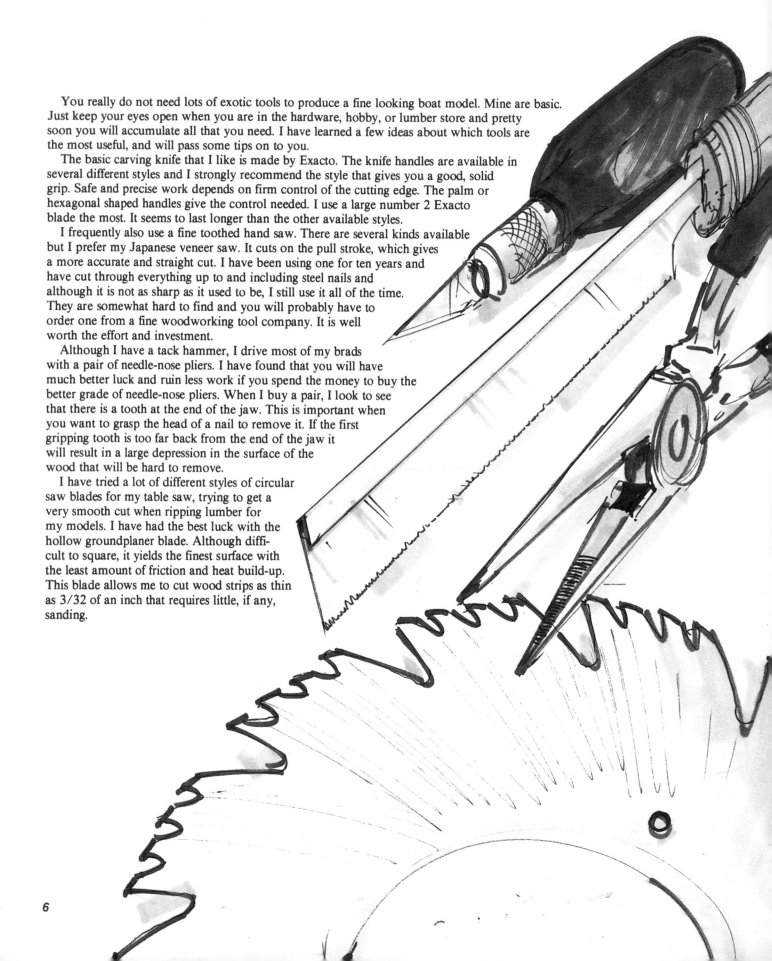

Paints and Brushes

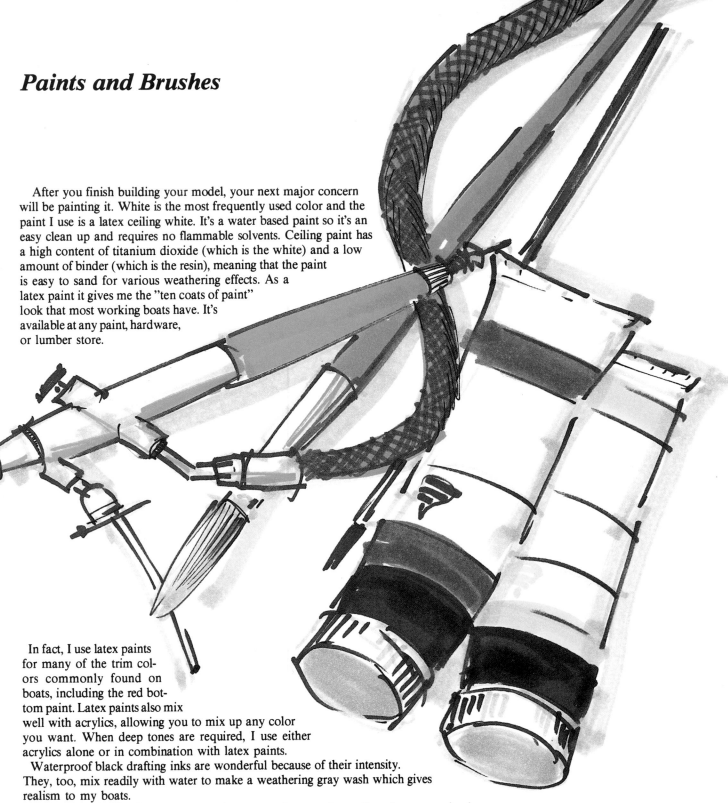

After you finish building your model, your next major concern will be painting it. White is the most frequently used color and the paint I use is a latex ceiling white. It's a water based paint so it's an easy clean up and requires no flammable solvents. Ceiling paint has a high content of titanium dioxide (which is the white) and a low amount of binder (which is the resin), meaning that the paint is easy to sand for various weathering effects. As a latex paint it gives me the "ten coats of paint" look that most working boats have. It's available at any paint, hardware, or lumber store.

In fact, I use latex paints for many of the trim colors commonly found on boats, including the red bottom paint. Latex paints also mix well with acrylics, allowing you to mix up any color you want. When deep tones are required, I use either acrylics alone or in combination with latex paints.

Waterproof black drafting inks are wonderful because of their intensity. They, too, mix readily with water to make a weathering gray wash which gives realism to my boats.

Solvent based paints in spray cans such as gray primer, and recently pale green and pale blue, prevent the water based paints from weakening the glue joints.

I use both conventional brushes and an airbrush. The brushes designed to be used with acrylics are best and I keep several sizes on hand. I use the airbrush as a miniature spray gun to give an overall wash when I apply the weathering effects. As with any other tool, it is important to keep all your brushes clean unless you do not mind buying lots of brushes.

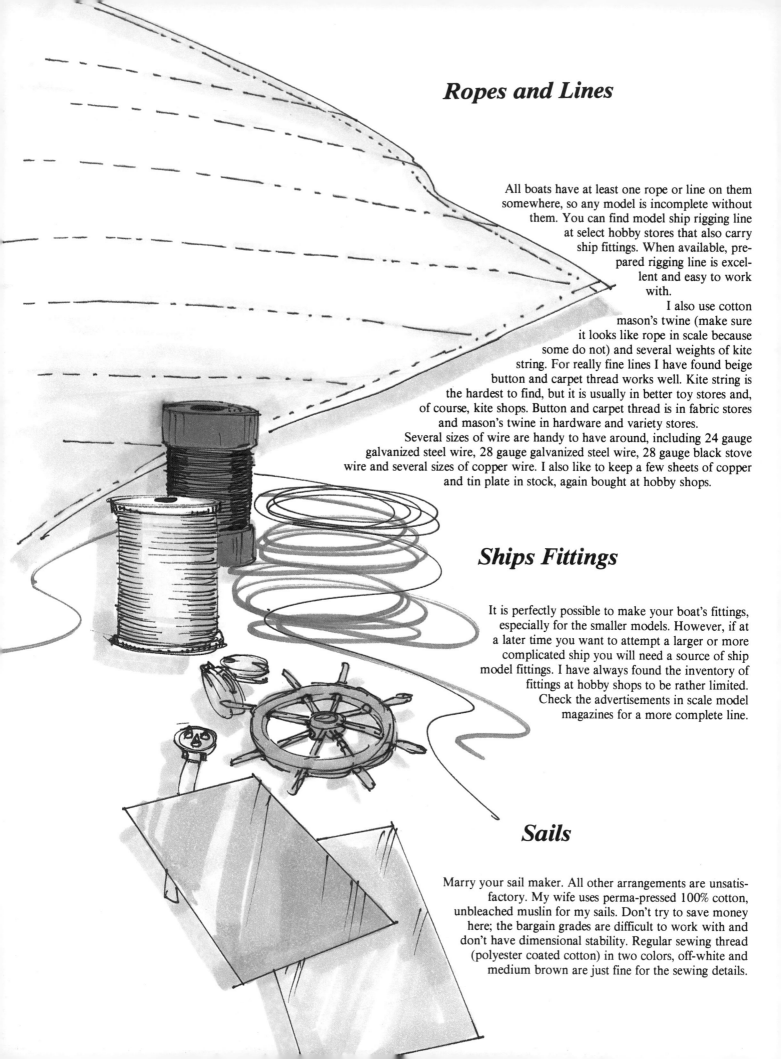

Ropes and Lines

All boats have at least one rope or line on them somewhere, so any model is incomplete without them. You can find model ship rigging line at select hobby stores that also carry ship fittings. When available, prepared rigging line is excellent and easy to work with.

I also use cotton mason's twine (make sure it looks like rope in scale because some do not) and several weights of kite string. For really fine lines I have found beige button and carpet thread works well. Kite string is the hardest to find, but it is usually in better toy stores and, of course, kite shops. Button and carpet thread is in fabric stores and mason's twine in hardware and variety stores.

Several sizes of wire are handy to have around, including 24 gauge galvanized steel wire, 28 gauge galvanized steel wire, 28 gauge black stove wire and several sizes of copper wire. I also like to keep a few sheets of copper and tin plate in stock, again bought at hobby shops.

Ships Fittings

It is perfectly possible to make your boat's fittings, especially for the smaller models. However, if at a later time you want to attempt a larger or more complicated ship you will need a source of ship model fittings. I have always found the inventory of fittings at hobby shops to be rather limited. Check the advertisements in scale model magazines for a more complete line.

Sails

Marry your sail maker. All other arrangements are unsatisfactory. My wife uses perma-pressed 100% cotton, unbleached muslin for my sails. Don't try to save money here; the bargain grades are difficult to work with and don't have dimensional stability. Regular sewing thread (polyester coated cotton) in two colors, off-white and medium brown are just fine for the sewing details.

The Workplace

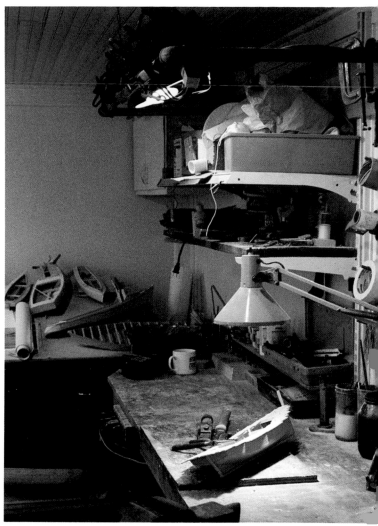

The conditions of your workplace are extremely important and a few considerations will make a great deal of difference in the enjoyment of building models. The first and simplest factor is lighting; there is no substitute for enough light. I use six 75 watt bulbs to cover my entire work surface. They are placed about four feet away from my table, and are set to shine down on the work area without shadows. Be sure you do not position them so you are staring right at them.

Your work surface must be firm and steady. If the surface can give when you apply pressure, slippage is possible, resulting in injury or damage to the model.

I choose to stand to work and my workbench is 36″ high, which is a comfortable height for me. I think it's safer to stand than sit; tools and pieces of wood do occasionally fall off, and being seated at the workbench puts your lap at risk.

Your workplace should be easy to clean up. Since you will be creating lots of chips, sawdust, filings, bits of wire and string, etc., you do not want carpeting underfoot. I stop and sweep up almost hourly to eliminate clutter. I have learned from experience, having lost a lot of time frantically searching for a tool that I desperately need. Of course it is right in front of me but I cannot find it in the mess.

One last important point: be prepared to handle a serious cut. Every boat I have made has a drop of blood on it somewhere. I keep a roll of paper towels and band aids on the shelf above my workbench.

Building a Small Rowing Skiff

Our project is a simple, basic skiff. I am sure many of us remember growing up owning such a skiff, using it to fish and explore. It's not hard to find such old, abandoned skiffs upside down and moldering away in marsh grasses. I found this particular skiff near the Kent Narrows on Chesapeake Bay; it's a good example. Some of its construction features are unique and we will incorporate them in our model.

Like most Chesapeake Bay boats it has a linered stem which means that it has an inside and an outside piece. This feature eliminates the necessity to rabbet the hood ends of the planks into a single stem piece. It also features an unusual departure from conventional construction technique in that it has a pieced chine log. The word "log" seems an unusual nomenclature for a piece of wood that reinforces the joint between the sides and the bottom but the term is derived from the same piece in the larger boats where it makes more sense.

This boat is about fourteen feet long and a little less than four feet wide. The side planks are 1″ x 10″ pine and the bottom planks are 1″ x 6″, fastened transversely across the bottom. The interior frames are 1″ x 1½″ on 16″ centers. The chine log pieces are approximately 3″ high with a beveled top (to prevent water from building up), and are fit between the frames.

We'll build our model in 1″ scale which means that 1″ equals 1′.

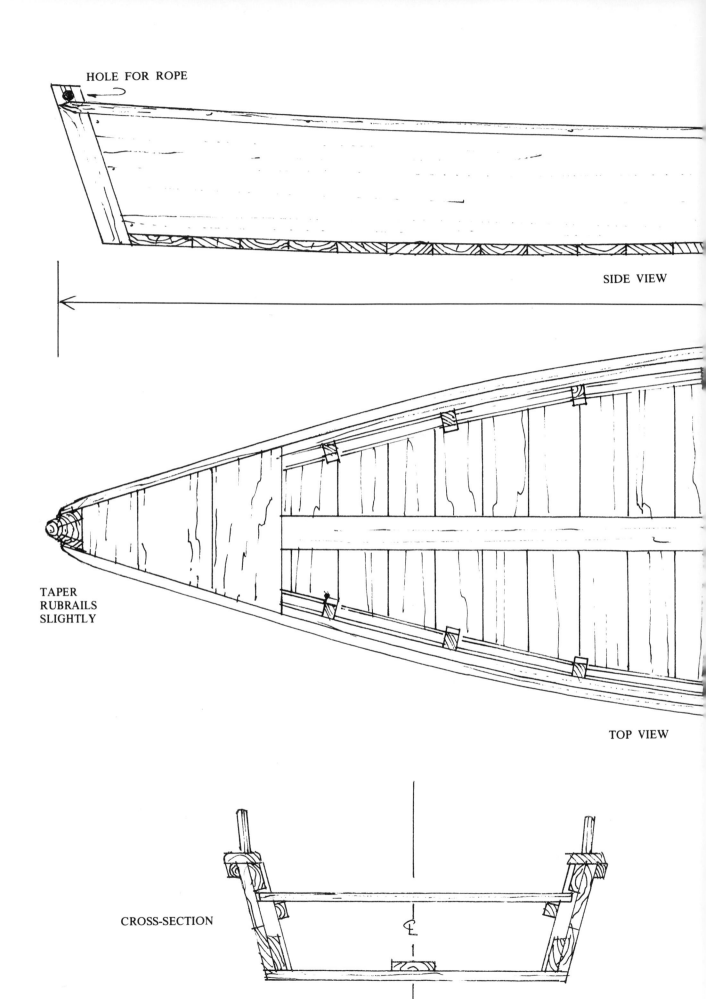

HOLE FOR ROPE

SIDE VIEW

TAPER
RUBRAILS
SLIGHTLY

TOP VIEW

CROSS-SECTION

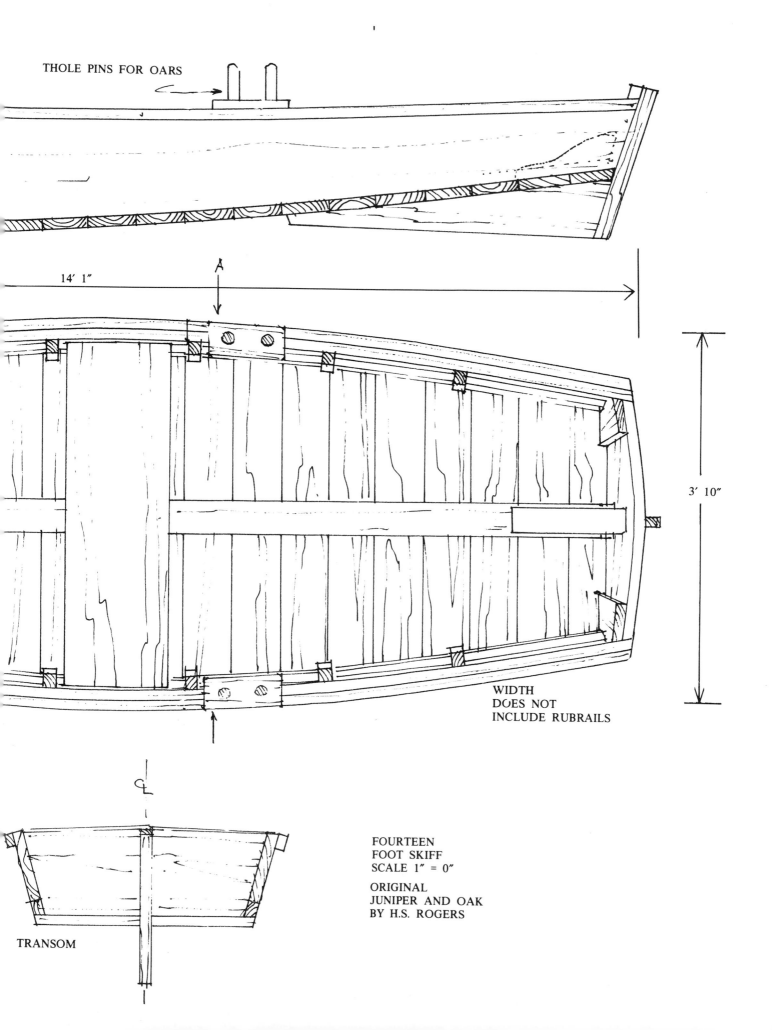

THOLE PINS FOR OARS

14' 1"

A

3' 10"

WIDTH
DOES NOT
INCLUDE RUBRAILS

TRANSOM

FOURTEEN
FOOT SKIFF
SCALE 1" = 0"

ORIGINAL
JUNIPER AND OAK
BY H.S. ROGERS

The stem and stem liner are cut from a ⅜" x ½" piece of white pine stock, 12" long. Both are carved at the same time. Each piece will be about 2" long, but don't cut them from your basic stock until you have finished cutting the bevel on both sides. Mark a center line on the ⅜" inch face and carve away the material between that line and the corner of the opposite face. Do this for about 5" down the 12" piece of wood.

Using a sanding block, sand the carved area lightly to remove any unevenness.

Repeat on the other side of the center line.

This shows the correct angle.

This is the result after the carving is finished.

After you have cut your bevels from both sides of the stock, cut off the first 2" to use as your stem liner and the second 2½" as the stem. The stem liner looks like this.

Build your transom. Use two pieces of ¾" x 3/32" pine stock about 4" long...

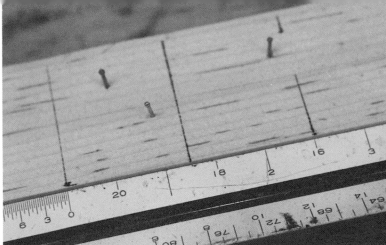

The width of the transom at the bottom is 2¼" to 2½". Measure out ½" of that width on each side of the center line; make a mark and establish a line.

and tack them into place with brads onto a small block of wood.

The transom has a small amount of flair so it will be wider at the top than at the bottom. Establish a point 3/16" beyond your two outside lines at the top of the transom.

Take your square and establish a center line.

Place a straight edge between the point at the top and the outside line at the bottom and draw a line above the edge. Do the same on the other side. This will give you the general shape of your transom. The bottom of your transom should now be 2¼" wide and the top 2⅝".

15

Now take a piece of white pine ½″ wide and 3/32″ thick and about 2″ long...

and lay a bead of wood glue onto the transom following the diagonal line.

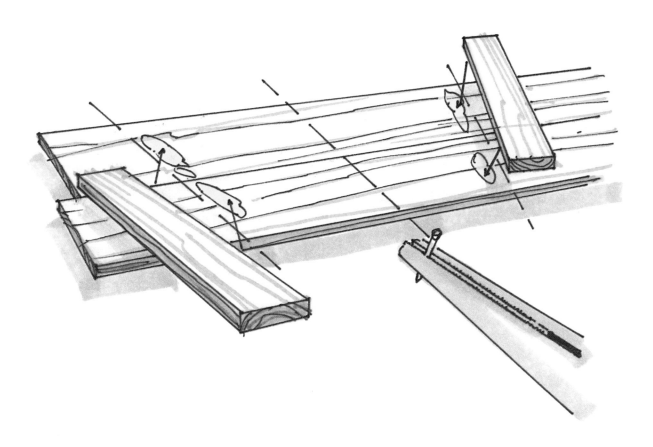

Use one piece for each side and two brads on each side to hold each piece in place until it dries.

Remove any excess glue. And set this piece aside.

Now you must select the side pieces for your skiff. The most important criteria is that the two pieces of ¾″ x 3/32″ strips 15″ long must be exactly the same thickness and as uniform as possible.

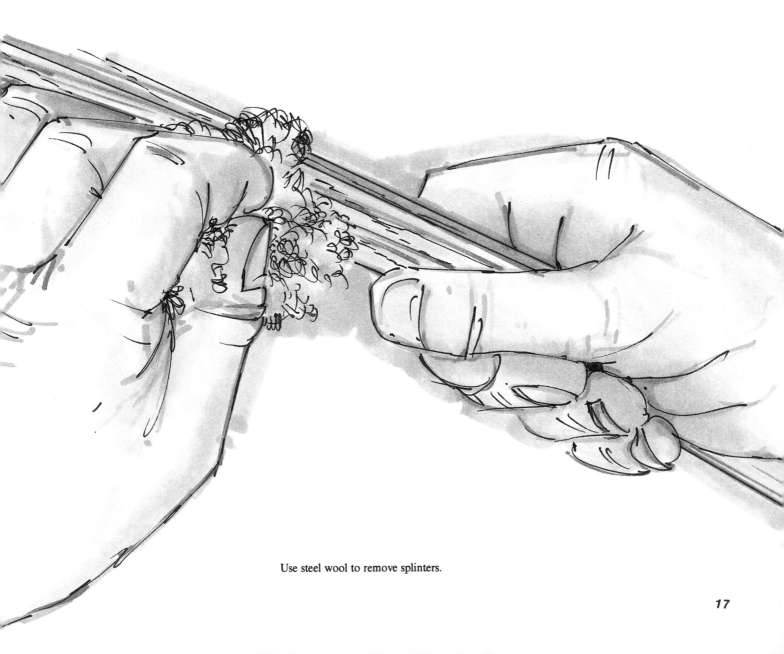

Use steel wool to remove splinters.

Place the two pieces together and drive a brad through the middle near each end.

After the first cut.

Cut one end at about a 75 degree angle.

Now measure from the first cut down the longer edge of the strips 13½″ and make a mark. Cut the board off at a slight angle, using the mark as the wider point. Discard scraps. This board should have angled cuts at each end that face inward. The long side is the top and the short side is the bottom.

On the back of the board that will become the stern mark a point ⅜ of an inch in from either edge. Measure a point on the bottom of the board that is in the middle of the short side of the board.

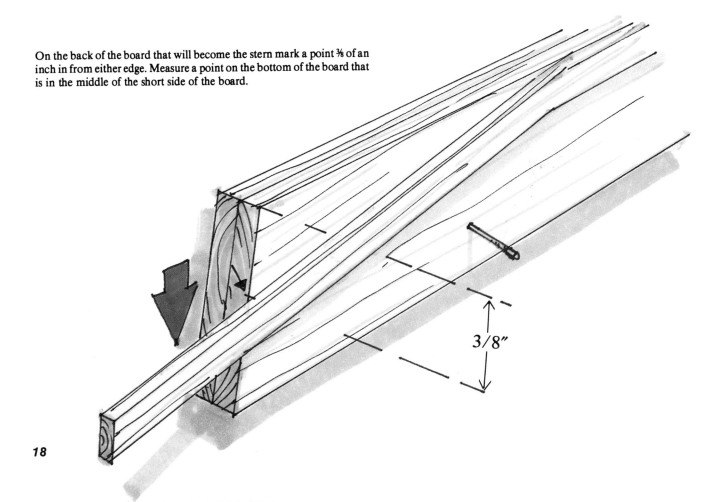

3/8″

Select a thin flexible piece of wood to use as a batten. Clamp the batten flush with the lower edge of the board near the center point.

Remove the clamps and the batten, take the board, put the top edge down on the surface of your work table, and plane away the material outside of the curved line.

Gently bend the stern end of the batten upward until the lower edge of the batten touches the ⅜″ point of the stern. This gives you the curved bottom of your boat.

Plane just to the line...

Mark a line from the lower edge of the board along the batten to the point in the middle of the stern.

and sand the length of the piece for a smooth edge. Remove the brads holding the two boards together and since both boards were cut and shaped at the same time, they should be identical. These are the lower side planks of your boat.

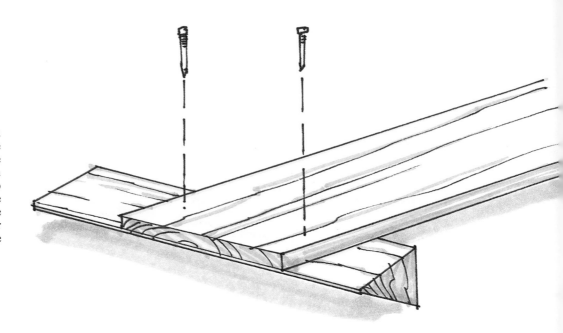

Pick up the stem liner and put a small drop of wood glue at the bottom of one of the faces and place the front end of one of the boards on this spot of glue. Carefully push two brads into the plank through the stem liner. Make sure that the forward edge of the stem liner matches the forward edge of the board.

It's okay for some of the stem liner to extend beyond the lower edge of the board because it will be trimmed later. Turn this assembly over so that the first board is flat on the work surface and the stem liner is on top of it. Put a drop of glue on the beveled face and press the other board onto the stem liner, making sure that the leading edge of the two boards are flush with each other. Take two brads and carefully press them through the boards into the stem liner.

Use a wet brush to wipe away any excess glue that squeezes out of the joint.

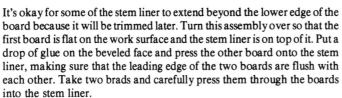

Pick up the assembly, looking at it carefully to make sure that the boards look even and balanced.

Redo this until it looks right because a mistake here cannot be corrected later.

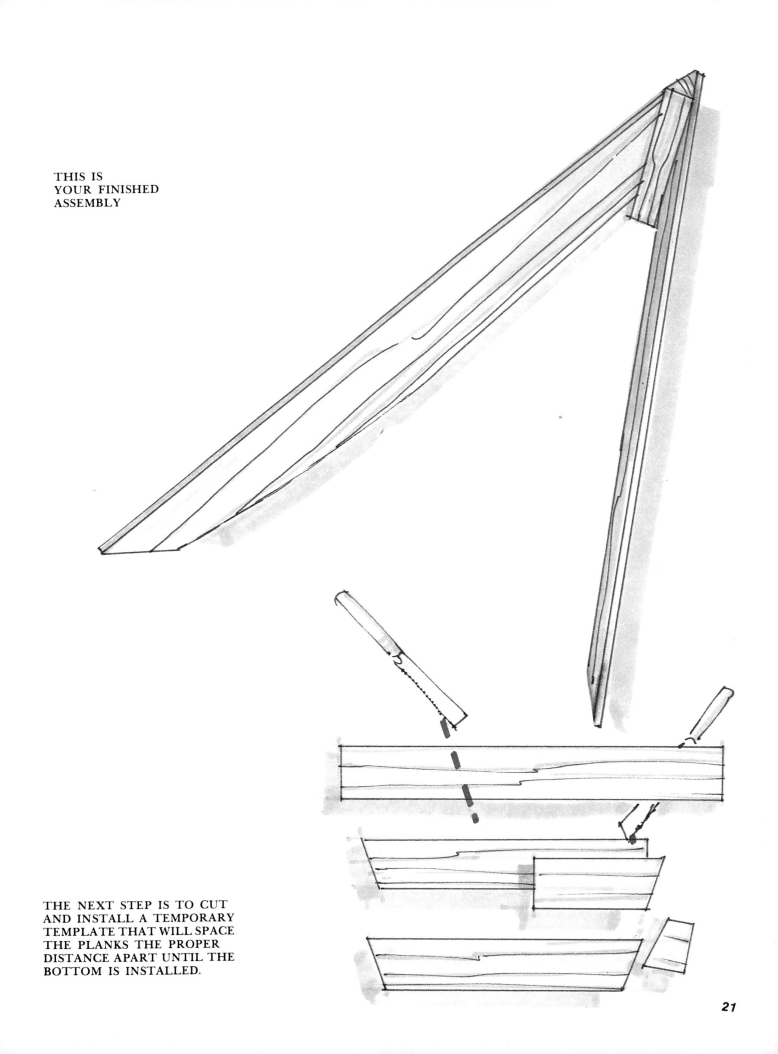

THIS IS
YOUR FINISHED
ASSEMBLY

THE NEXT STEP IS TO CUT
AND INSTALL A TEMPORARY
TEMPLATE THAT WILL SPACE
THE PLANKS THE PROPER
DISTANCE APART UNTIL THE
BOTTOM IS INSTALLED.

Cut a template that will keep the sides apart at the proper width while we attach the bottom planks. We will use a piece of white pine ½″ x ¾″ approximately 6″ long to make the template. This template will be nailed into the boat during the building process and removed when the boat is finished. This piece should be shaped like the drawing. The bottom measurement will be 3½″. Make a cut with a slight angle on it at a point two inches from the end of the 6″ piece of wood.

Mark a point 3½″ away from the first cut. Copy the first angle you cut on a piece of scrap and cut it. Lay the scrap piece on the template and mark the angle so that the short length is 3½″. This is how you insure that your angles are equal. Discard the scrap and saw on the line through the template.

You now have a template; set it aside.

Now we'll attach the transom to the lower side planks, using the template to establish the basic shape of the boat. Begin by removing the transom from the block of wood.

Sand a bevel on either side of the transom making sure that the bevel is on both the frame and the planks of the transom. Make certain that the end result is very smooth...

Saw away any excess wood on the sides...

and flat. Do this on both sides.

and from the top and bottom.

Reattach the transom to the block of wood, with the outside face down.

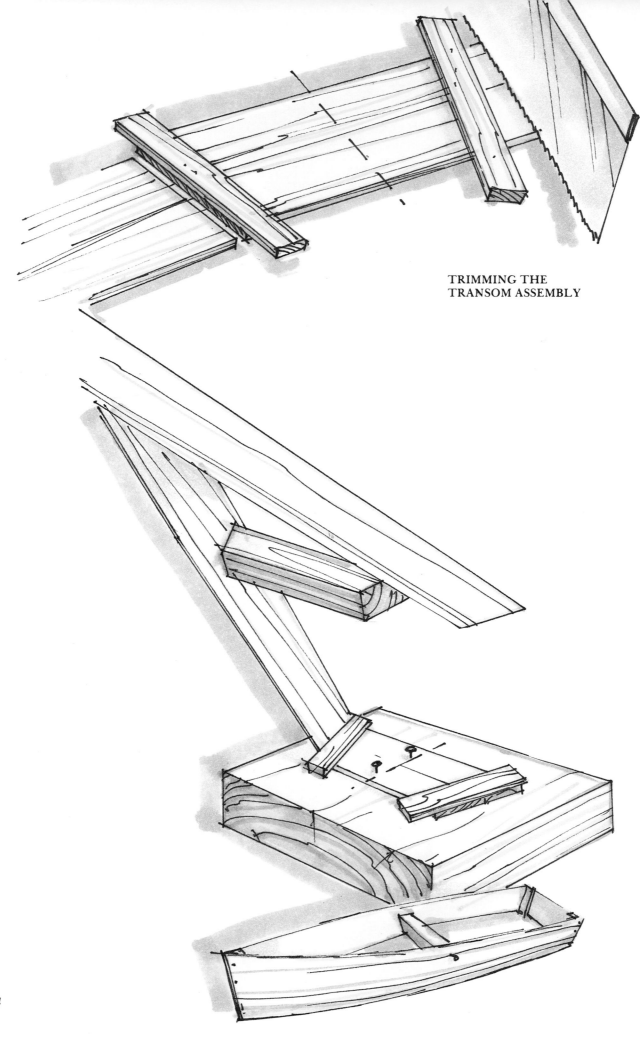

TRIMMING THE
TRANSOM ASSEMBLY

Take the right side of the stem and side plank assembly and put a drop of glue on the inside face near the stern. Place the stern end of the right side of the assembly against the left side of the transom. Line up the lower edge of the lower plank with the bottom edge of the transom.

Carefully drive two brads through the side plank into the frame. At this point the side plank should appear to be attached to the transom at a slight angle. The joint should be tight and secure. Using a wet brush, remove excess glue. Repeat with the other side plank.

Put some glue on the left lower side plank and inserting the template amidship, bend the left lower side plank around and fasten it to the corresponding point on the right side of the transom. Drive two brads in to secure the joint.

Position the strongback template. Carefully put two temporary brads through the two lower side planks into the template.

To establish the final and correct alignment of the template, measure a point on each side equidistant from the stem. This point should be fairly close to where the template is now. The lower edge of the template should be approximately ⅜″ above the lower edge of the side planks so that it does not interfere with the attachment of the chine pieces. Carefully withdrawing the brad from one side at a time, position the template at the previously established points.

Look at your work from all angles to make sure that it is not warped or unbalanced. Inspect the transom joints to make sure they are still sound. Allow the assembly to dry thoroughly before proceeding.

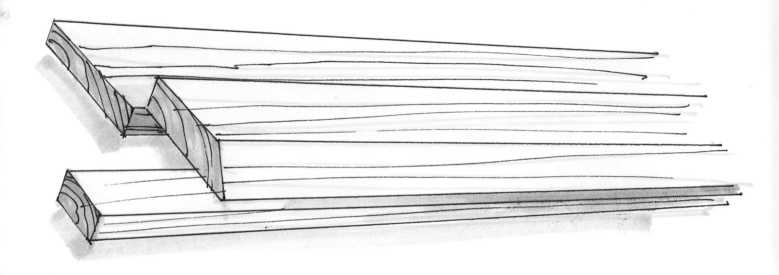

Cut the pieces for the frame and chine out of white pine. Use your table saw to cut three or four pieces two feet long and ⅛″ x 3/32″ for the frames. Next, cut three or four pieces ⅜″ wide with a 30 degree bevel on one side for the chines, and one piece with no bevel for the keelson. Cut about twelve pieces 3/32″ x ½″ wide about two feet long to use as bottom planks.

Cut sixteen pieces 2″ long from your ⅛ x 3/32″ stock and set aside.

Pick up the sides and the transom assembly (from here on referred to as "the boat"). Using one of the chine pieces, slide it up against the stem on the inside of the boat, noting the angle at which it must be cut to fit flush against the stem. Also notice that a slight bevel must be sanded on this cut in order to accomplish a completely flush fit.

Using a ruler, measure one piece of your chine material 1¼″ long. Make sixteen pieces, making sure they are identical to the first. Set aside.

This shows the marked angle.

The completed cut...

and the sanded bevel...

Make a small pool of glue on a scrap of wood (for applying glue to the frames).

give a nice flush fit against the stem. Run a bead of glue on the inside face of the lower side plank along the lower edge, beginning at the stem.

Beginning at the stem, place the first chine piece over the bead of glue, pressing it into position against the stem and secure with a clothespin. Make sure that the lower edge of the chine piece is flush with the lower edge of the boat. Pick up a side frame piece, apply glue to the edge and position it at the end of the chine piece, perpendicular to the upper edge of the board. The frame may project below the edge of the board piece; it will be cut later. Follow the frame member with another chine piece. Position against the lower edge of the board. Repeat the steps until you get to the stern of the boat. If the template interferes with the placement of the frames, interrupt the process and reposition the template.

The last chine piece will have to be trimmed to fit against the transom frame. This joint will be visible, so be careful.

If the frame pieces appear to need clamping, do so. Repeat the process on the other side of the boat.

Another view of the last chine piece fitted and in place. The last piece should show ⅛″ below the side plank.

When both sides are done, hold it up and check the alignment of the frames. Make any adjustments now. Look at the top edge of the side boards to check for glue blobs (if they are not removed, planking will be difficult). Set the boat aside to dry.

Using a stiff brush dipped in water, carefully remove any glue that has oozed out of the joints.

Select two 2¾″ x 3/32″ planks, inspect for uniformity and cut a piece slightly longer than the boat. Apply glue to the face of the stem liner, all of the frames, and don't forget the transom frame. Position the plank on the boat so that it covers the entire length of the boat. Push the front end of the plank against the stem liner and fasten it with a brad.

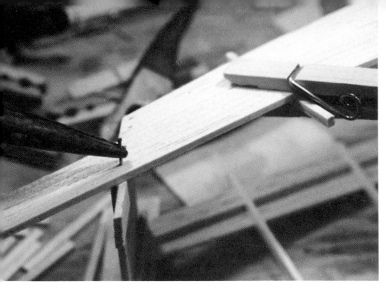

Repeat the procedure at the transom.

The assembly should look like this.

Clamp the plank to the side frames with clothespins.

Trim the board to the stem and the stern and repeat the procedure on the other side. Check to make sure that each plank is pressed firmly down against the plank below it.

Brush away excess glue.

Add additional brads to the stem.

Remove oozing glue and set aside to dry.

Trim the plank ends when the assembly has dried.

When dry, trim away any side frames that extend above the top plank.

Turn the boat over and trim any of the side frames that extend below the chine.

Trim off the stem liner...

and the transom frames.

The finished assembly from the top.

The bottom view.

Using a sanding block with coarse paper, place the block across both chines and gently sand both chines at once the length of the boat. Be especially careful at the transom pin that the sandpaper does not catch on the bottom. I usually turn the sanding block at a slight angle to prevent this. Sand the bottom slowly and gently. There's no rush.

Continue sanding until you have produced a smooth surface on the chine pieces, the frame, and the lower side pieces. Check for a fair curve by looking down the length of the chine on each side.

To establish the equidistant points needed to lay the bottom planks, tack a short piece of batten to the bottom of the stem with a brad.

Sand out any inaccuracies in the transom. You will glue the bottom pieces to this surface. The transom view of the sanded bottom.

Swing it to each side like a compass and mark a point first on one side...

Remove the fuzzy surfaces with steel wool.

Then the other.

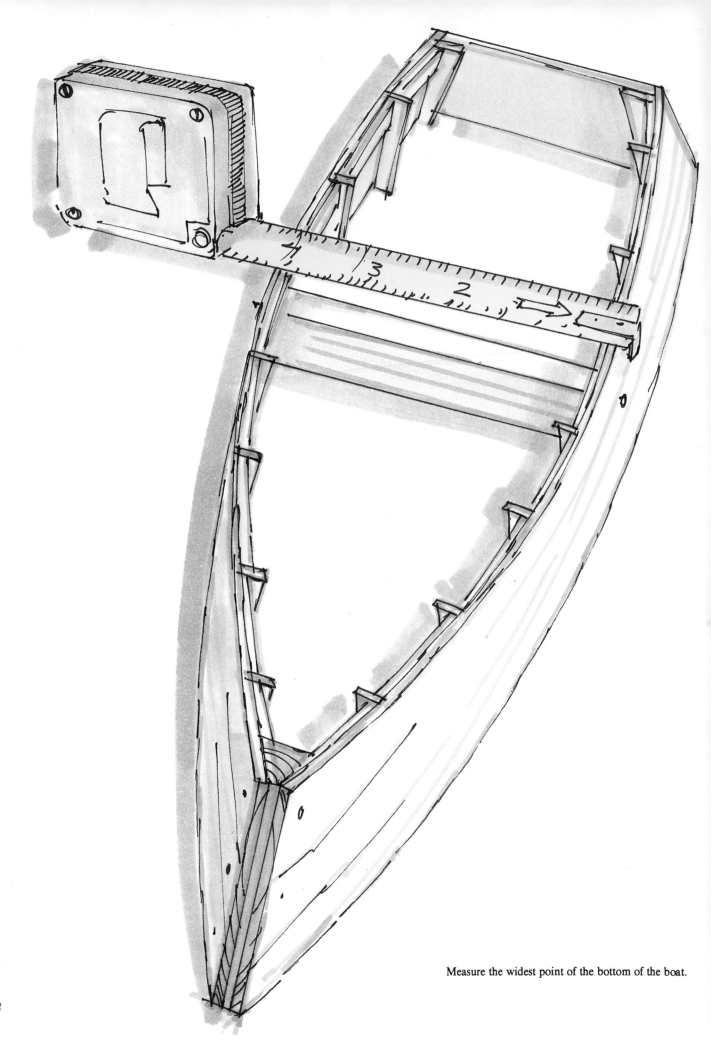

Measure the widest point of the bottom of the boat.

Using fine steel wool or sandpaper, go over each bottom plank piece to eliminate any splinters or fuzz from cutting.

Run a bead of glue along the entire length of the chine on both sides.

Begin placing the bottom planks starting at the equidistant points.

Take the ½″ x 3/32″ strips of wood (bottom planks) and cut enough bottom plank stock to cover the bottom of the boat into pieces about ½″ longer than the widest point of the boat bottom.

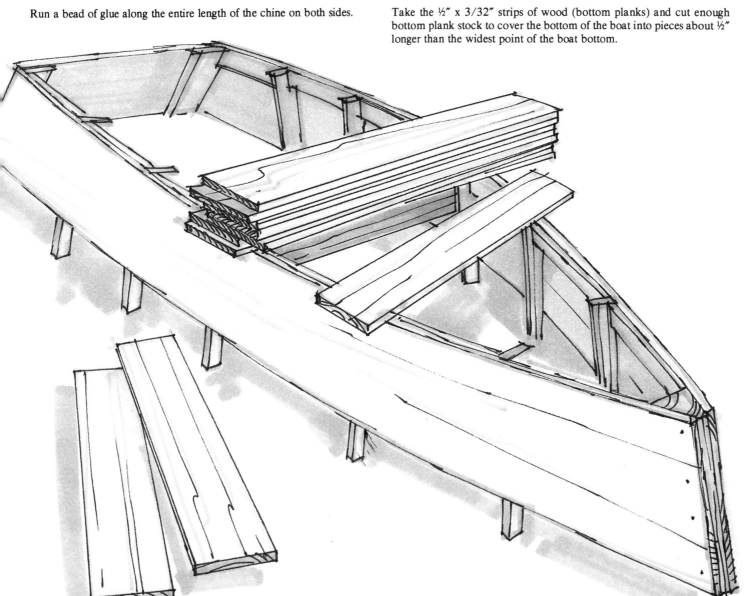

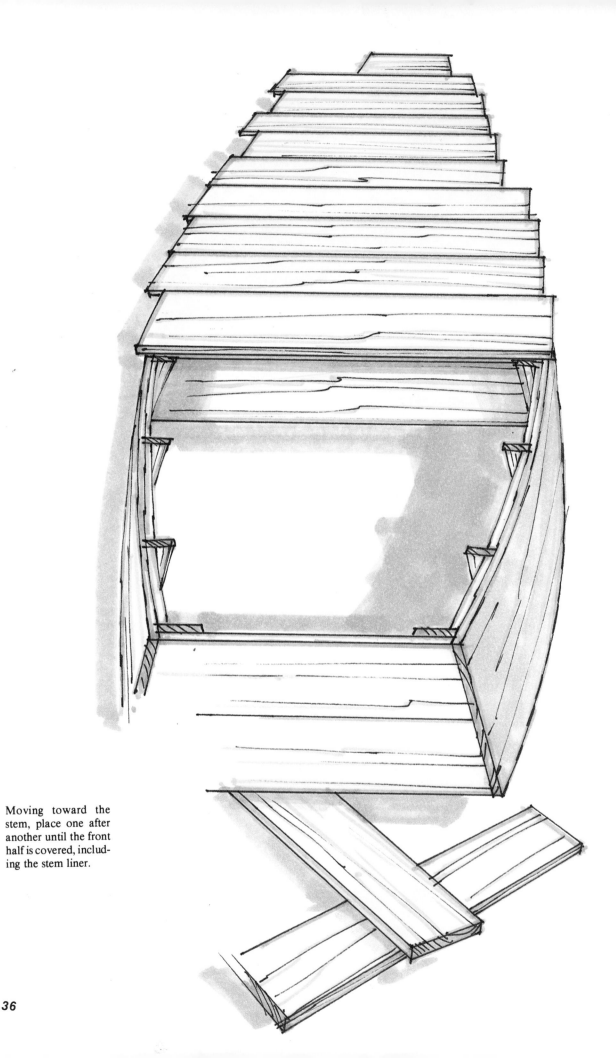

Moving toward the stem, place one after another until the front half is covered, including the stem liner.

Turn the boat over and holding the planks in place with your hand, gently remove any glue on the inside of the boat with a brush.

After drying the boat looks like this.

Complete the rest of the bottom.

When dry, remove the center template brace...

Brush away any remaining glue. Turn the boat back over and gently press on the bottom planks to insure firm contact. Set the boat aside to dry.

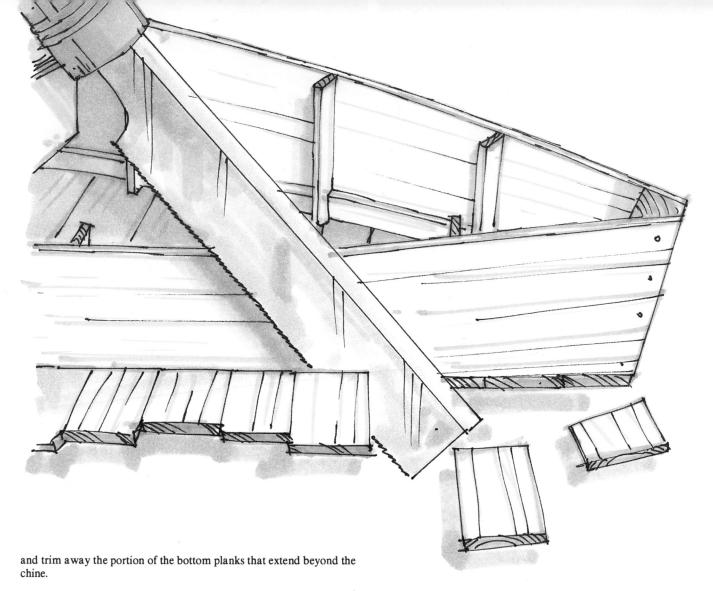

and trim away the portion of the bottom planks that extend beyond the chine.

Cut as close to the side planks as possible, but keep a fraction of an inch away from the sides to avoid scoring them with the saw blade teeth.

The trimmed bottom should look like this.

Sand the bottom edge.

and the face of the stem.

I use shadows to find areas that I have missed in the sanding.

Next we take the piece of wood we reserved for the keelson. Holding it in place, determine where it must be cut to fit snugly into the stem of the boat. As you can see, it will need to be tapered and slightly beveled.

Sand the bottom surface...

Using a knife carefully trim it to fit between the stem and chime pieces. Bevel the front edge to follow the angle of the stem with the sanding block.

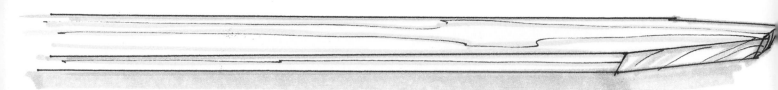

It should be shaped roughly like this.

Refit it into the stem.

A good fit will require a slight bevel.

With the keelson in place in the stem, make a preliminary cut to fit along the bottom of the boat, and butt against the transom at the centerline.

Check the fit of the keelson. Remove the keelson, apply a bead of glue and put back in the boat. Secure to the bottom of the boat at several points with brads. Check for excess glue and remove.

Using a piece of batten tacked into the stem...

mark two equidistant points on each side two inches from the stem. These will be for the deck.

Make shallow cuts at the marks, approximately 3/32″ deep.

With your saw, start at a point on the stem that is slightly less than 3/32″ down from the top and saw in a straight, parallel line back to the first cuts.

HERE IS WHAT MAY BE
A CLEARER PICTURE OF
THE PROCESS. . . .

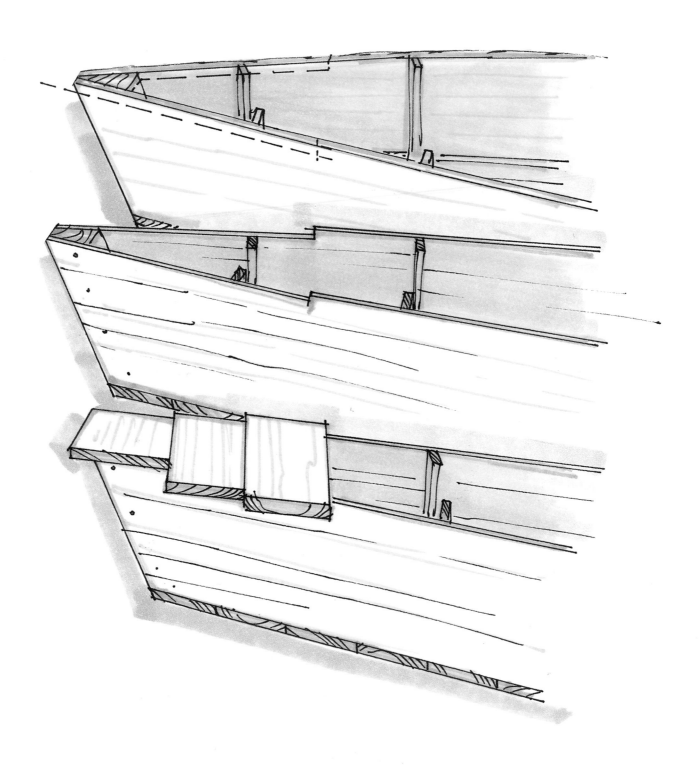

Do this on both sides and remove excess stock.

Run a bead of glue along the top edge of each plank.

The finished cut.

Apply decking plank material starting at the first cut and moving toward the stem. Remove any excess glue and set aside to dry.

Use your knife or sanding block to correct any irregularities.

Remove the brads from the keelson

When dry, trim away any excess planks extending beyond the sides of the boat.

Glue the second piece that was cut from the beveled stock and attach it to the sanded surface of the stem. Allow to dry.

The trim should be close.

When dry, trim only the bottom of the stem.

Use the sanding block to smooth all deck plank ends so that they are flush with the side planks. Continue to sand the foredeck, the keelson (after the brads are removed), and the bottom of the boat. Lastly, sand smooth the forward surface of the stem liner and side planks so that it's straight and perpendicular to the center line of the boat.

Sand this bottom cut.

It is likely that the stem piece will be somewhat wider than the width of the bow of the stem. If so, trim the piece with a knife.

Use a piece of 3/32″ x ⅛″ stock for the rub rail. Glue and temporarily hold it in place beginning with the stem, using clothespins as temporary pins.

Sand it until it is flush with the side planks.

Pin at both ends. By gluing before pinning, the rub rail is held in place making the pinning easier.

The sanded stem.

Repeat on the other side.

When the glue is dry trim the front ends of the rub rail...

Sand lightly.

like so.

Mark the middle four frames of the boat about ½″ below the top of the side plank. Use a ½″ piece of wood as a guideline.

Trim the rub rail at the transom.

Glue and fasten a piece of frame stock to the frames horizontally, covering the middle four frames of the boat at the marks, and continuing under the deck.

This will serve as a support for the seat boards.

Some boat builders fit a small knee to support the transom. The angle is identical to the one between the bottom and the outside edge of the transom. Use a piece of ⅜″ x ½″ stock; hold it along the bottom to the transom. Place another small batten across the transom and mark a line where the batten crosses the ⅜″ stock. Cut the ⅜″ stock at this point. Make a second cut 1″ away from the first and using your Exacto knife, shape the knee brace. Glue in place.

Use a piece of chine stock to fit between the frames at mid-ships and create the thole pin support. Glue it with the beveled side down and the upper edge flush with the top of the side plank, and clamp in place. Use spring clamps to create the pressure needed to fit this piece to the curve of the side plank.

Fit two pieces of 3/32″ x ¾″ stock across the seat supports. Cut them so they fit snugly inside the side planks. Use your sanding block to create the necessary bevel.

Repeat on the other side.

Glue them in place.

Remove the sequin pins and clothespins from the rub rail and using your sanding block, sand the entire upper edge of the side plank and rub rail until they are even.

Some skiffs have a small keel at the back. Glue a small piece of frame stock in the center of the transom and extending below the transom about ¾″.

At the point where you glued the piece of chine stock between the frames, glue two short pieces of wood about ¾″ wide x 3/32″ thick centered on the seat.

When dry, turn the boat over and, using a 4″ long piece of ¾″ x 3/32″ stock, hold it alongside of the frame stock approximately in the position it would be for the keel and mark a line where the frame stock crosses the keel.

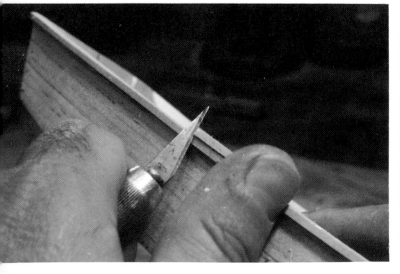

These are the thole pin blocks. When these are dry, trim them off flush with the edges of the sides.

Mark the profile of the boat bottom on the keel piece.

Trim away the excess.

Check the fit of the keel again and either whittle or sand away enough material so that it will fit snugly against the bottom.

Cut the end of the keel along the line you drew.

Glue in place, and brush away the excess glue.

Reposition the ¾″ stock against the forward edge of the frame stock, making sure that it is accurate. Make another cut about 3″ away from the stern at a slight angle. Draw a line from a point ⅛″ above the forward cut to the aft end of the first cut. Cut along this traversing line.

Fasten the keel with a sequin pin at the forward end.

When dry, sand away any excess material and shape the profile of the keel.

Trim the excess

Drill two 3/32″ holes in each thole pin block.

Drill a hole in the stem for the line.

Glue and insert a round toothpick for the thole pins.

This is the boat so far.

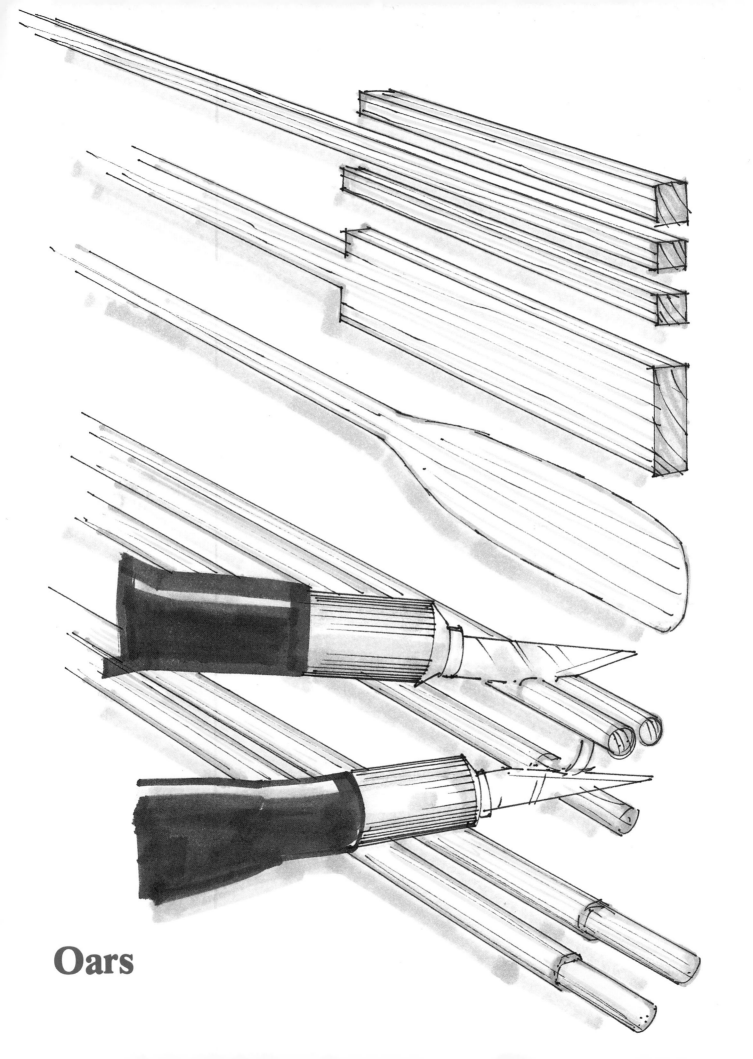

Oars

On your table saw, cut three or four pieces of wood ¼″ square about two feet long.

When dry, use your plane to shape the end into the flat curved oar blade.

Cut two pieces 8″ long from this stock and then cut four pieces 3″ long.

Cut back the shoulder of the blade on the shaft on each side.

Glue the 3″ pieces on opposite sides of one end of the 8″ stock.

Use your plane to round the shaft of the oar.

Holding the oars at the shoulders, sand the blade end of the oars until they match each other.

Follow with the sanding block to complete the final shaping.

Using your knife, mark the handle end of the oar to make each oar the same length. Roll the oar on the work surface under the knife blade until the cut is complete.

Sand the final taper into the oar.

Again holding the oars together, mark a second point ¾″ from the end of each oar, for the hand grip. Gently roll the oar underneath the knife blade on the work surface, making a shallow cut all the way around. Shave away slivers of wood from the end of the oar to this shallow cut, creating the hand grip. Lightly sand the oars to eliminate any surface irregularities.

Hold both oars together and line up the shoulders.

The finished oars.

Painting Your Boat

Spray the inside with a flat gray primer.

and paint the bottom red, tinted to look like bottom paint. Try to avoid runs. If it happens, as it did here, let it dry, then sand or scrape away and repaint.

Paint the outside planks and transom white with a large acrylic brush and latex paint.

When dry, mask the sides of the boat...

When you remove the tape some of the paint will come off the sides of the boat, helping to give it the aged look we are after.

The rub rail, the fore deck, the top edge of the stem and side plank, and the transom are painted dark blue.

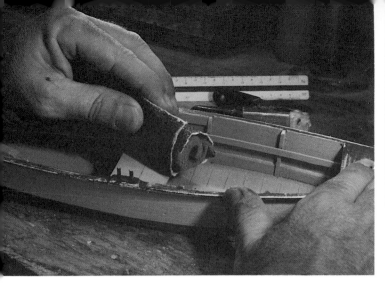

Wrap a piece of coarse sand paper around a short piece of foam insulation (the kind used for water pipes), and sand away the edges of the frames, chine, seat, and keelson.

Again a small piece of paper will get into the hard to reach places. The sanding produces a nice weathered effect and is one of the trademarks of my skiffs.

Get into tight places with a small folded piece of sandpaper.

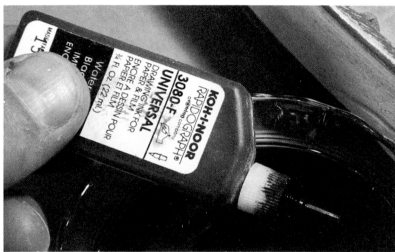

Make up a solution of gray wash, using warm water and black drafting ink.

Lightly sand the dark blue areas, removing only the edges and occasionally sanding through the finish. Lightly sand the sides and transom as well as the bottom.

Test the solution on wood scraps until the stain produced is a medium gray. Dip or paint the oars in this solution.

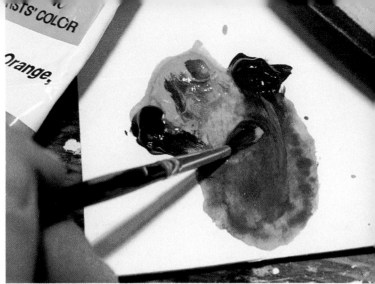

Finish your model by first brushing the entire surface of the boat inside and out with clean, fresh water.

Make a very thin solution of acrylic paint, using burnt sienna, burnt umber, and orange (mixed with water to thin it down) until it looks like rust. Using a small, fine brush, touch a few places on the boat while it is still wet where rust would appear, mainly wherever iron fasteners are under the paint such as the hole pins at the top of the stem and at points near the transom.

Now dip your brush in the ink solution and brush liberally over the boat, inside and out.

Rinse the brush out, dip it in clean water and brush away any build-up of ink solution that looks too dark.

Discoloration from rust will also appear inside the skiff any place that water would pool. However, beware of allowing water to pool up in your model; if it does, pour the water out by way of the transom. When your model is dry, you can repeat the weathering process if necessary. Many of the colors will have lost their intensity as they dried and a second application will add more depth.

Take an 18″ length of mason's twine and soak it in the same solution. When dry, tie the twine through the hole in the stem. Coil it around one finger and thumb and drop the coil into the skiff.

The boat with rope and oars.

Carve one end of a short piece of ½″ x ½″ stock to fit in the hole.

Model Base

I prefer mounting my boats on pieces of driftwood rather than on bases bought at hobby shops. Not only is the driftwood more natural looking, it is also more graceful in form. Part of the fun in building boat models is scrounging the shoreline for suitable pieces. My wife and I particularly enjoy walking along the beach in the fall and winter, enjoying the wildlife and the chance encounter with the perfect piece of driftwood. I have quite a collection outside of my studio door; storing the driftwood outdoors does no damage.

To make your base, drill a ⅜″ hole in the middle of a stable piece of driftwood.

Insert in the hole...

Glue the piece in place and use a brush dipped in gray solution to simultaneously wash away excess glue and stain the post.

Drill a ⅛" hole in one corner of your driftwood base

Hold your skiff over the base and determine by eye the most attractive height. Trim the mounting post accordingly.

Insert some tall grass (I find the grass I use along railroad tracks). Determine the right height and cut it accordingly.

Put a drop of glue on top of the mounting post. Position the boat and fasten with several small brads. Triangulate the angle of insertion of the brads to increase their holding power.

The mounted boat.

Glue it in place.

Gallery of Model Boats

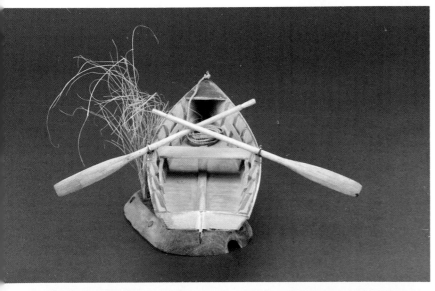

The Kent Narrows rowing skiff.

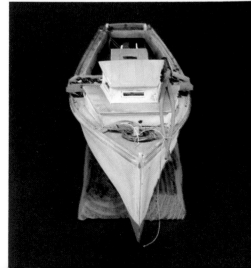

Hand tong, dead rise Chesapeake Bay launch.

The modeled engine of the Chesapeake Bay launch lies under the removable housing.

Hooper's Island launch with a drake tail stern.

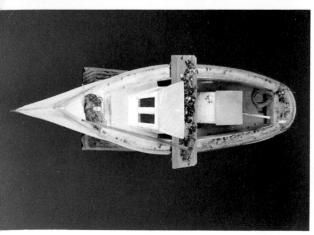

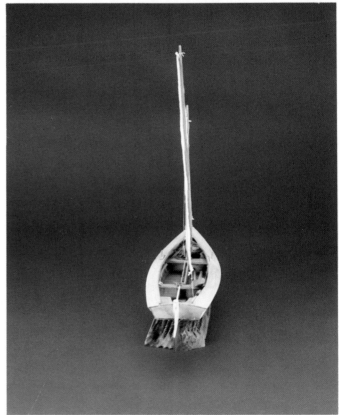

North Carolina sailing flat bottom skiff.